THE TRIANGLE SHIRTWAIST FIRE

On Saturday, March 25, 1911, a fire broke out in the eighth-floor factory of the Triangle Shirtwaist Company in New York City. It lasted only about thirty minutes. But unsafe working conditions and poor fire laws contributed to the deaths of 146 people. Out of the disaster came a great cry for reform.

PRINCIPALS

THE 146 VICTIMS OF THE FIRE, mostly young women.
MAX BLANCK and ISAAC HARRIS, owners of the Triangle Shirtwaist Company.

Ruins of the Triangle Shirtwaist Company. (United Press International)

The Triangle Shirtwaist Fire, March 25, 1911

The Blaze That Changed an Industry

by Corinne J. Naden

Illustrated with photographs and contemporary prints

FRANKLIN WATTS, INC.
845 Third Avenue, New York, New York 10022

The authors and publishers of the Focus Books wish to acknowledge the helpful editorial suggestions of Professor Richard B. Morris.

For Aunt Inza and Uncle Frank,
with love

Other Focus books by the author:
The Chicago Fire
The Haymarket Affair

Cover photograph courtesy *Brown Brothers*
Maps and diagrams by Walter Hortens

Contents

THE TRIANGLE SHIRTWAIST FIRE

After the fire; looking out a window of the Asch Building onto the fire escape. (Brown Brothers)

CHAPTER 1

The Fire

The time was 4:45 P.M., Saturday, March 25, 1911. The place was the Triangle Shirtwaist Company, located on the eighth, ninth, and tenth floors of the Asch Building, Greene Street and Washington Place, New York City. The happening was a fire.

The Triangle fire began in a rag bin on the eighth floor. It lasted about thirty minutes. And it caused the death of 146 Triangle workers, most of them young women. They were burned to death as they sat at their worktables. They were burned because they could not open a locked door in time. Many died as they jumped to the sidewalk, one hundred feet below. Others died when they jumped down the elevator shafts.

When it was over, horrified people had questions to ask. How could so many die so quickly in a building that was said to be fire-proof? Why was the country's largest and most modern city unable to save them? Where was the four-thousand-man fire department, with its high-pressure system and aerial trucks? Who was to blame?

Some of the questions were fairly easy to answer. People died

New York's firemen on the job in 1911. (Brown Brothers)

quickly in the Asch Building because it was not fireproof at all. The New York Fire Department was on the scene within minutes after the fire broke out. But for all their equipment, it was simply not enough. In a city of emerging skyscrapers, the New York Fire Department could not fight a fire effectively above the seventh floor.

[4]

However, the fire department did have some of the latest equipment, including a fourteen-foot rope net. It was stretched out over the sidewalk, and three girls jumped into it from the ninth floor. They hit the net with a force equal to sixteen tons. The net was torn out of its frame, useless. The girls died.

Other questions were not so easy to answer. What laws allowed a firetrap to be declared fireproof? Why were doors locked in the Triangle Company? And most of all, who was to blame for the deaths of 146 people?

Were the owners of the Triangle factory to blame? Hadn't they ordered the doors to be kept locked? Were the owners of the Asch Building to blame for operating a firetrap? Was the city of New York to blame for its almost nonexistent fire laws? Were labor laws to blame for not protecting workers against overcrowded and unsafe sweatshop conditions? Or did they all share in the responsibility?

Like most tragedies, the Triangle fire might have been forgotten once the horror of it faded from people's minds. But it was not forgotten. In a sense it never has been. For the fire in the Triangle Shirtwaist Company actually changed the clothing industry. It influenced factory laws for years to come. It brought new regulations involving sanitary and safety conditions. It was responsible for a new fire prevention law and for the organization of a division of fire prevention.

The fire in the Triangle Shirtwaist Company did something else, too. It made the public wake up. People were horrified at what had happened. And they demanded to know the causes. If the public had not demanded to know, the Triangle fire might have been forgotten as just another unfortunate disaster.

[5]

CHAPTER 2

Work in the Sweatshops

The clothing industry in the United States today employs over one million workers. A century and a half ago, there was no clothing industry at all. Most clothes were made at home and by hand. Although the more wealthy women could afford to have cloth imported from Europe, the average woman wore homespun material called linsey-woolsey.

In 1846 Elias Howe, an inventor from Massachusetts, patented the sewing machine, which led to the growth of the clothing industry. But Howe must share the credit with a New York inventor, Isaac Merrit Singer. Howe's sewing machine required the operator to turn a crank wheel with her right hand. Therefore, the sewer had only one hand free to work. Singer's machine, invented in 1851, was operated by a foot pedal, leaving both hands free.

After these two inventions, the clothing industry began to grow. At first most of the cloth was cut by dealers and sewn at home by woman employees. They made only outer garments — coats and cloaks. As the demand grew, the industry had to expand into fac-

Sweatshop conditions in New York City. (Brown Brothers)

tories. By 1860 there were nearly two hundred clothing factories, mostly in New York and Pennsylvania. Over five thousand people were employed, most of them women. They did everything from cutting out the patterns to packing the clothes for shipment.

It did not take long for the clothing factories to become sweatshops. A sweatshop is a business that employs workers under unfair and unsafe conditions. Working conditions in the clothing factories were very poor. They were overcrowded and barely ventilated. The lighting was bad. Most women earned from one to three dollars a week. There was no such thing as an eight-hour workday.

But the industry continued to grow as people more and more demanded manufactured clothing. The women's wear industry was far less important than the men's and would continue to be until 1914. By that time the sale of women's wear had overtaken that of men's clothing, and it still outsells men's wear today.

Many craftsmen came to the United States from Europe during the latter part of the nineteenth century. They entered the growing American clothing market. In 1880 the cutting knife was invented. Since use of the cutting knife required a fair amount of strength to slice through many layers of material, men began to take over the cutting work. The women remained as sewers.

All during the last half of the nineteenth century, workers in the clothing industry tried to fight sweatshops and other unfair working practices. During this period workers in all industries used strikes and violence in an effort to gain better wages, hours, and working conditions. Unions were organized and began to exert some power. By 1911, the year of the Triangle fire, there were 736 unions in New York City alone.

In April, 1891, a group of forty-seven delegates from clothing unions in New York, Boston, and Philadelphia held a convention. Out of it came the United Garment Workers of America (UGW). Nine years later a separate national organization was founded for women's wear workers. It was called the International Ladies' Garment Workers Union (ILGWU), and in 1900 it boasted two thousand members.

Both the UGW and the ILGWU belonged to the American Federation of Labor (AFL), then the major labor organization in

[8]

Samuel Gompers (right) talks with David Holmes, British labor leader, at AFL convention in 1894. (United Press International)

the United States. (The AFL merged with the Committee for Industrial Organization — CIO — in 1955.)

The AFL had grown out of a cigarmakers' union headed by London-born Samuel Gompers. He became the AFL's first president, in 1886. Craft unions in both the United States and Canada belonged to the AFL. Its aim was to gain shorter hours, higher pay, and better working conditions for all employees. But it was not an easy fight.

For instance, in 1904 the National Credit Association of Clothiers organized a bureau to bring in the open shop. The open shop is a factory in which workers are free to decide whether or not to join the union. The closed shop is a factory in which only union members may be hired.

The UGW objected to the bureau set up by the clothiers. A strike was called, eventually involving 25,000 clothing industry workers. But despite the union's efforts, the strike was a failure in Chicago and New York. The clothiers refused to bargain with the union and refused to fire nonunion men.

In 1910 the ILGWU, with an association of cloak manufacturers, set up the Joint Board of Sanitary Control. Its purpose was to get rid of sweatshops in the industry, something it tried to bring about over the next fifteen years.

For a long time, the law did very little to help the American worker. In the latter part of the nineteenth century there were few laws against child labor or the employment of women in coal mines. Four states of thirty-eight in the Union at the time gave factory workers any protection at all against unsanitary conditions or fire hazards. The blacklist and the ironclad oath were in use. The blacklist contained names of troublemakers — usually workers involved with a union. It was circulated among business owners. Anyone on the list would not be hired. The ironclad oath was a statement that workers were made to sign in order to get a job. It said that the worker would not join a union. And there were many other unfair practices. Women clothing workers, for example, were charged part of their salaries to pay for the sewing machines they worked on.

It is true that by the time of the Triangle fire, clothing workers had made some progress over the years. The unions were stronger and had brought about some easing of sweatshop conditions. The year before, the clothing union had won a major strike in Chicago. As a result, minimum wages were set at five dollars a week and the

[10]

Garment workers on strike in the early twentieth century. (United Press International)

work week at the company was reduced to a mere fifty-four hours.

But that was only one firm in Chicago. By 1911 most of the clothing workers still had to endure poor working conditions, salaries, and hours. Factories were unsafe and unsanitary. And, above all, there was the ever-present danger of fire. The Triangle Shirtwaist Company in New York City was a perfect example of a factory of the time.

CHAPTER 3

The Triangle Shirtwaist Company

Charles Dana Gibson was an artist and illustrator. On the staff of *Life* magazine, he made himself famous in the late 1890's by introducing the "Gibson girl." He sketched what the public came to regard as the ideal American woman. Gibson girls wore high-necked blouses, called bodices or shirtwaists. With full, billowy sleeves and tight waists, they were considered the last word in fashion. Shirtwaists had mannish-type collars and were usually worn with tailored skirts.

By the early 1900's, the shirtwaist and tailored skirt had become the "uniform" of the bright, emancipated working girl. She was pictured as crisp and efficient, and not fussily feminine, despite the fact that shirtwaists were usually made of flimsy, see-through materials.

Thanks in good part to the Gibson girl, the Triangle Shirtwaist Company was a booming concern in 1911. In fact, it was the largest business of its kind. Its more than five hundred employees, most of them young women (the youngest was about fourteen), spent six

The Gibson girl figure.
(United Press International)

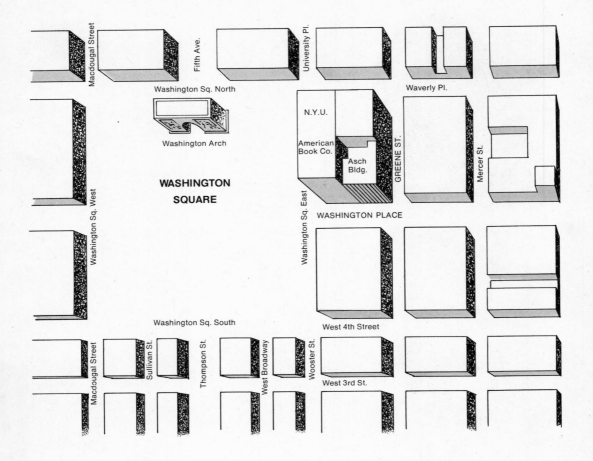

days a week turning out shirtwaists in all fabrics and colors. Often newly arrived in the United States, the girls had no fixed starting salaries and few raises.

The Triangle Shirtwaist Company filled the top three floors of the Asch Building, on the corner of Washington Place and Greene Street in New York City. Greene Street was one block east of Washington Square Park, once a burial place for the city's unclaimed dead. But Washington Square had become a fashionable area in lower New York during the nineteenth century. New York University and the American Book Company, in the same block as the Asch Building, faced the park.

Washington Square was no longer quite so fashionable in 1911. Industry and immigrants were slowly approaching the row of old, picturesque town houses that lined the north side of the park.

The Asch Building was ten years old at the time of the Triangle fire. In 1902 the Triangle Shirtwaist Company had moved into the ninth floor, and by 1908 it also occupied the eighth and tenth floors.

Washington Square, looking north, early twentieth century. (Brown Brothers)

Triangle was owned by Max Blanck and Isaac Harris, who had grown wealthy in the shirtwaist business. Blanck took care of the "outside" duties, such as entertaining buyers. Harris ran the factory. They left the hiring, firing, and paying of employees to their supervisors, and often did not know how many people worked for them at any given time.

The two underlying causes of the Triangle disaster were the fact that the Asch Building was a firetrap and the fact that the Triangle Shirtwaist Company was a sweatshop.

The plans for the Asch Building had been approved by the city of New York. According to the fire laws of the time, the building was fireproof. It had wooden floors and wooden window frames. The law said that stone floors and metal frames were necessary only in an eleven-story or higher building. The Asch Building had ten floors. But New York City's fire chief had stated in 1910 that his men could successfully fight a fire only up to seven floors.

The Asch Building, however, was not alone. In 1911 about half of New York's over 500,000 workers spent their time above the seventh floor.

According to fire laws, if a building had 10,000 square feet on each floor, it also had to have three staircases on each floor. The Asch Building had 10,000 square feet but only two staircases (each less than three feet wide) per floor. The city overlooked this because the building did have a fire escape, leading to a court in the back. However, the fire escape ended at the second floor.

According to labor laws, factory doors had to open out and could not be locked during working hours. The Asch Building was planned so that all the doors opened in. And the doors on each floor of the Triangle Company were usually locked during the workday.

[16]

Asch Building, 1911. (United Press International)

The company felt this was necessary to keep track of so many employees and to prevent stealing of material.

It was not that these hazards went unnoticed. In 1909 the Asch Building had been inspected, and it was noted that the doors were locked and the top floors too crowded. Nothing was done. A year later, the fire department inspected the building and reported it in good condition. It was once again declared fireproof.

So, the owners of the Asch Building were not totally to blame. They had more or less obeyed the laws and had been allowed to continue as before. That, however, should not really be surprising. The city did not set much of an example. In 1911 New York had no laws that required fire escapes in factories, no laws that required fire drills, and no laws that required fire sprinklers. A report issued shortly before the Triangle fire showed that 99 percent of all shops in the city were below safety standards and 94 percent had doors that opened in. Only one company out of all in the city had ever had a fire drill.

In 1910 the Women's Trade Union League investigated a fire in Newark, New Jersey, that killed twenty-five people. It made recommendations for fire safety standards in New York City buildings. A New York University professor reported fire hazards in the Asch Building, which he could see from his classroom across the court. A city politician pushed for an investigation of fire and safety laws in factories. All were ignored.

The Asch Building and the Triangle Shirtwaist Company had seen fires before 1911. In 1902 two fires broke out, both on the ninth floor, and there were fires in 1908 and 1909. Small fires were not uncommon. At the time of the 1911 fire, the Triangle Company carried almost $200,000 worth of insurance. What they collected after the disaster amounted to about $500 for every worker killed.

[18]

If the Asch Building had cause to be called a firetrap, the Triangle Shirtwaist Company could be termed a sweatshop.

Certainly, conditions at the Triangle were unfair, even if they were not particularly unusual for the time and place. The girls had no fixed beginning salary rate, no promise of raises. Their salaries could be determined entirely on the whims of the supervisors. Their hours were long and dreary. Their pocketbooks were checked every night at quitting time to make sure they weren't stealing anything. To complain was to be fired.

Work conditions at the Triangle were also unsafe and unsanitary. In 1909 an inspection had noted that the top floors were too crowded. A New York law said that every factory worker had to have at least 250 cubic feet of air. But it didn't say where the air had to be. The Asch Building, like other buildings in the city, had very high ceilings. Workers could be crowded together on the floor and still have 250 cubic feet of air above each of them.

Besides the fire hazards of the building itself, the workers sat at wooden tables on wooden chairs. The sewing machines dripped oil, and everywhere lay bundles of flimsy, combustible material. The only way to fight possible fire was to use some of the 259 pails of water scattered around the building's ten floors.

The Triangle owners had a history of trouble with labor. In 1908, after a strike protesting working conditions, Blanck and Harris allowed a "company union" to be formed. One out of five workers was eligible to join. However, within a year all of the union members had been fired. The remaining girls at the Triangle Company appealed to the ILGWU. In September, 1909, another strike was called, and some two hundred Triangle workers walked off their jobs.

[19]

A typical textile factory, 1910. (Brown Brothers)

In answer, Blanck and Harris brought in police. The girls on the picket lines were sometimes beaten and often carted off to jail. This treatment gained much public sympathy for the garment workers and led the ILGWU to call a general strike. By December, there were 20,000 striking shirtwaist workers, and the shutdown had spread to Philadelphia.

Two months later the strike was over. The union had won some gains for its members, one of them being a fifty-two-hour workweek. But the girls at the Triangle Company had won nothing. Blanck and Harris would not recognize the union and would not allow a five-and-a-half-day week. The doors still opened in. The fire escape still ended at the second floor. And the stage was set for the twenty-fifth of March.

CHAPTER 4

Eighth and Tenth

It was Saturday afternoon, March 25, 1911, and close to 4:45 P.M. — quitting time. On the eighth floor of the Asch Building, the Triangle Shirtwaist employees were finishing up for the day. The floor, as always during working hours, was crowded.

The Triangle's eighth floor, just like the ninth and tenth, was about one hundred feet square. All along the south wall stood a row of closely spaced sewing machines. Twelve windows on this wall overlooked Washington Place. On the west wall, which faced the American Book Company and New York University, were two passenger elevators and one of the two staircases. Next to the staircase, a partition hid the dressing room and washrooms for the girls. The indented northwest corner had three windows, and there were eight windows along the north wall, looking down into a court. The two middle windows led to the fire escape. Two cutting tables ran parallel to the north wall.

The northeast corner of the eighth floor was also hidden by a partition. Behind it were two freight elevators and the second stair-

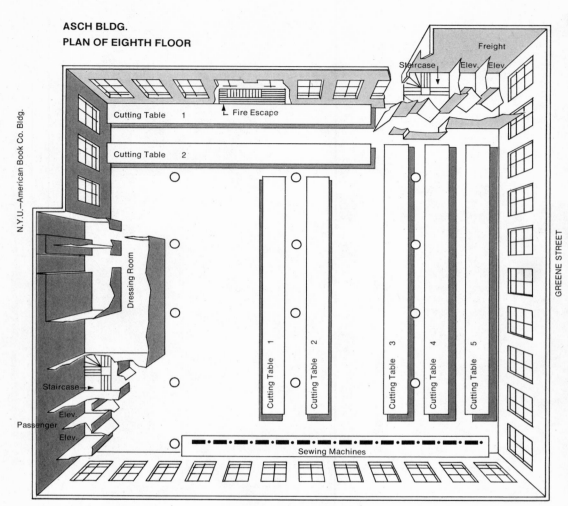

ASCH BLDG.

PLAN OF EIGHTH FLOOR

N.Y.U.–American Book Co. Bldg.

Cutting Table 1

Fire Escape

Cutting Table 2

Staircase

Freight

Elev. Elev

Dressing Room

Cutting Table 1

Cutting Table 2

Cutting Table 3

Cutting Table 4

Cutting Table 5

Staircase

Elev.

Passenger

Elev.

Sewing Machines

GREENE STREET

WASHINGTON PLACE

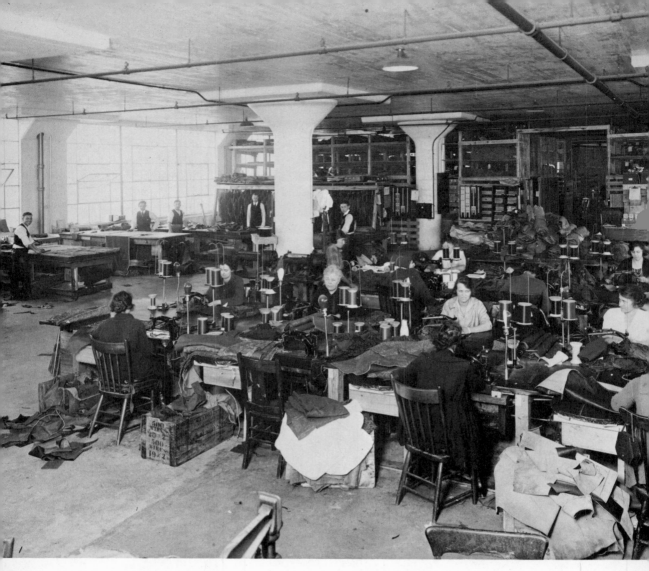

Textile workers. Note cutting tables at far left. (Brown Brothers)

case. A watchman stood by the partition each night, checking the girls' pocketbooks as they filed past, to make sure no scraps of material were taken home.

The east wall, facing Greene Street, had ten windows. Parallel to them, and filling up a large part of the floor, were five cutting tables. Three tables took up about two-thirds the length of the room; the other two were somewhat smaller. Some forty cutters worked at these tables.

Cutters were an extremely important part of the shirtwaist business. Good cutters knew the best way to place patterns on material, saving the owners money by getting the most out of the fabric. With one slice, a cutter went through dozens of layers of material on the table before him. The cut-out pieces were hung on overhead wires, to be given to the girls at the sewing machines. The scraps were stuffed in large bins under the tables. From time to time, an outside dealer would come in and cart away all the scraps. The last time this had been done was the middle of January. It was now nearing the end of March.

When the quitting bell rang, the girls began to leave for the dressing room. One of them suddenly noticed smoke coming from the bin under the second table on the Greene Street side. She yelled for the superintendent, while some of the cutters immediately tried to put the fire out.

Superintendent Samuel Bernstein grabbed pails of water and ran to help. Some of the girls did the same. A fire in one of the bins was not all that unusual, and many had been put out quickly.

No one knew how the fire started — perhaps a spark or a match — but this one spread with almost unbelievable speed. (Smoking was not allowed at the Triangle Company, although the rule was not enforced.) Flames leaped to catch the pattern pieces overhead and

[25]

consumed the cloth-filled bins under the tables. Piles of flimsy material quickly began to burn, filling the room with thick smoke.

Bernstein yelled for the hose, but it was rotten and fell off the wall. There was no water pressure anyway. Windows began popping from the heat.

By now, Bernstein realized that he could not put this fire out. He began to yell for the cutters to help get the girls out safely.

There were three choices of escape — the elevators, the fire escape, and the stairs. Some of the workers rang frantically for the elevators. Indeed, before the fire was over, the men running both the passenger and freight elevators would be overcome by smoke and exhaustion as they made trip after trip to rescue as many as possible.

Some of the cutters and about twelve of the girls chose the fire escape. The fire escape steps were more like those of a ladder and a number of people fell from landing to landing. One man fell into the court. Some of the girls fought their way down to the sixth floor and broke windows to get in there. All in all, the fire escape saved only about twenty people out of over five hundred on all three floors.

The rest of the girls tried to go down the narrow, winding stairways. Those who rushed for the Washington Place staircase found the door locked. After much screaming, someone got it open — inwardly — and there was panic and confusion as the girls tried to pour out into the narrow stairway. At the seventh floor, someone fell. Those behind just began to pile up, until there was no room in the stairway for the women still on the burning eighth floor.

A policeman, who by this time had seen the fire and had run up the Washington Place stairs, managed to unsnarl the block of frantic women at the seventh floor. About 125 girls stumbled down the stairs to safety.

Moments after the fire had been spotted on the eighth floor,

[26]

Looking down the fire escape. Note top of picture, where fire escape gave way. (Brown Brothers)

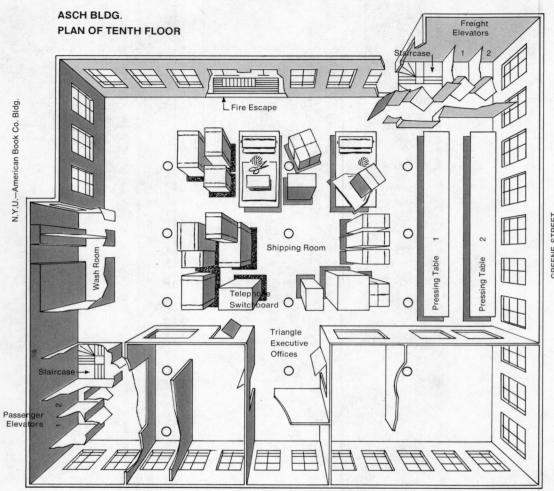

ASCH BLDG.
PLAN OF TENTH FLOOR

N.Y.U.—American Book Co. Bldg.

Freight Elevators

Staircase

1 2

Fire Escape

GREENE STREET

Wash Room

Shipping Room

Pressing Table 1

Pressing Table 2

Telephone Switchboard

Triangle Executive Offices

Staircase

Passenger Elevators

1 2

WASHINGTON PLACE

Diana Lipschitz, the bookkeeper, had called in the alarm. Then she attempted to warn both the ninth and tenth floors. No one answered the phone on the ninth floor, but she did get through to the tenth.

The tenth floor of the Asch Building contained the Triangle's executive offices, which ran all along the south wall. About forty men and women worked at the pressing tables lined up against the east, or Greene Street, wall. Almost the entire rest of the tenth floor was occupied by a huge shipping room, filled with packing cartons and other shipping materials.

The company switchboard was also located on the tenth floor. The regular switchboard operator was out that day, and when the substitute received the call from Diana Lipschitz, she did not believe her report. However, a quick check of the Greene Street stairway, now filled with smoke and fire, soon convinced her. She sounded the alarm and then abandoned the switchboard to find her father, the tenth-floor watchman.

Both of the Triangle's owners, Blanck and Harris, were in the office that day. Blanck had brought his two daughters, aged five and twelve, to work with him. All in all, about seventy people occupied the tenth floor at quitting time. Except for one girl, who immediately jumped out of a window in fright, all were saved.

As soon as the alarm sounded, Harris began to push girls toward the Washington Place elevators. The elevators that went all the way to the tenth floor were filled immediately and could not stop for passengers on the ninth or eighth.

Superintendent Bernstein ran up the stairway from the eighth floor to the tenth a few minutes after the fire started. He guided most of the people, including Blanck and his children, to the roof. By doing so, he saved their lives.

On the tenth floor of the adjoining New York University building, a law class was in session. Immediately after the fire began, professor and students saw the flames and heard the screams. They quickly ran to the roof of their building, which stood about fifteen feet higher than the roof of the Asch Building.

By incredible good luck, painters had left their ladders on the roof of the university building after completing work that day. The students used the ladders as bridges to the skylight of the Asch Building. By forming a line, they helped to guide the frightened victims across to safety.

As the last of the tenth-floor occupants reached the university roof, smoke and flames were leaping all about them. And, in fact, fire did cross to the New York University building. Students and teachers had to rush to the law library to carry out the books.

Despite fright and confusion, most of the people on the eighth and tenth floors of the Triangle Shirtwaist Company survived the fire. Their co-workers on the ninth were not so lucky.

CHAPTER 5

Trapped on the Ninth

About 260 people were working on the ninth floor of the Triangle Shirtwaist Company that Saturday in March. Less than half
would live through the afternoon.

The ninth floor was filled with sewing machines. Eight double
rows of sewing machines stood next to each other on continuous
tables — 240 machines in all. They filled almost the entire floor. The
only other things in the room were the partitions that hid the dressing room and elevators. The windows, elevators, and staircases were,
of course, in the same positions on the ninth floor as on the eighth
and tenth.

The sewing tables were seventy-five feet long. They held fifteen
machines on each side. The only way to leave the rows of tables was
at the north end. The girl sitting at the first machine on the Washington Place wall had to walk the entire length of the row in order
to exit.

Each worker had her own few feet of space. She sat on a
wooden chair, working at a wooden table. A basket of flimsy ma-

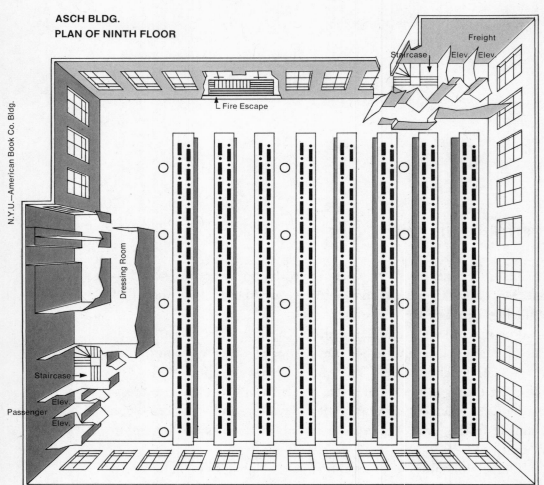

ASCH BLDG.
PLAN OF NINTH FLOOR

N.Y.U.—American Book Co. Bldg.

Freight

Staircase Elev. Elev.

L Fire Escape

Dressing Room

GREENE STREET

Staircase

Elev.

Passenger

Elev.

WASHINGTON PLACE

terial stood at her feet. A small bowl to catch the oil drippings from her machine was hooked just above her knees.

The first ninth-floor worker to see the flames was a young man named Max Hochfield. When the switches had been shut off for the end of the workday, he had quickly grabbed his coat and headed for the Greene Street stairs. The other workers were still slowly shuffling up the narrow aisles to the cloakroom or the elevators. But Hochfield was in a hurry. He headed down the stairs and suddenly saw that the eighth floor was in flames.

Those still on the ninth floor did not know a fire had started until the flames began leaping in the windows. The telephone never rang to sound a warning. By the time the fire had reached the ninth floor, it was almost too late to escape. In the first two or three minutes after the alarm was shouted, about 150 people raced for the Greene Street exit. They fought each other to get past the narrow

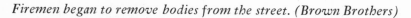

Firemen began to remove bodies from the street. (Brown Brothers)

partition. More than a hundred of them made it to the sidewalk below. Everyone else was trapped inside.

Some of the girls ran for the Washington Place door. It was locked. No one could open it. But it really wouldn't have mattered. By now the fire had filled the entire stairway leading up from the eighth floor.

Some tried the fire escape. But the smoke was so thick on the outside stairway that it was almost impossible to see. But that did not really matter much either. In a few minutes, the fire escape, by now jammed with people, pulled from the wall and collapsed. The bodies fell into the courtyard below.

Some were too frightened to do anything at all. They burned to death at their worktables.

Some rang for the elevators. But the ninth floor had been the last to get word of the fire. By the time they called the elevators, the cars were already being filled with people from the eighth and tenth floors. Almost all the elevator operators stayed in their cars until they were nearly dead from smoke and exhaustion. But it wasn't enough for those on the ninth. When they could not get in the elevator cars, the girls tried to slide down the elevator ropes. Some simply jumped down the shafts. Later, many bodies were found together at the bottom of each elevator shaft. Some landed on top of the elevator cars themselves. When their weight became too heavy, the elevators caved in.

For the rest of the people on the ninth floor, there was only one way to escape the flames. They jumped out of the windows. Of course, there was little chance that they could have survived the hundred-foot jump to the pavement. But they had a choice of jumping or burning to death. Most of them jumped. The impact of falling

The impact of falling bodies broke through the concrete and glass pavement. (United Press International)

bodies was so great that it smashed holes in the concrete and glass pavements.

By the time the fire department arrived, the girls were already crowding in the windows and out on the ledges. There was no way to save them. The nets quickly proved useless. In their fright, the girls jumped in twos or threes, arms entwined, rather than alone.

[35]

Their combined weight just tore through the nets. Firemen stood helplessly as bodies fell about them. Within a few minutes, the street was covered with the dead and dying.

If the fire department could not save them, what was it doing?

The first alarm for the Triangle fire had been turned in by John Mooney, who happened to be walking by the building around 4:45 P.M. The fire department responded quickly, eventually sending thirty-five pieces of fire-fighting equipment. The first to arrive was the horse-drawn pump engine of Company Eighteen.

But the city also sent its most modern equipment to fight the Triangle fire, including some of the department's first motorized units. The Asch Building was part of a newly set up high-pressure area. This system allowed extra water pressure to be built up at certain hydrants.

Hook and Ladder Company Twenty arrived with the tallest ladder in the fire department. Raised by a hand crank, it reached to the sixth floor. The fire department had warned that it could fight fires effectively only to seven floors. Now it was proving the truth of those words.

The nets were of no use. The horses that pulled the fire-fighting equipment were becoming frightened by the smoke, screams, and flames. The ladders were not high enough to rescue anyone. Hoses were taken up inside the building to prevent the fire from spreading to the lower floors. But all the firemen could do outside was to aim the hoses over the heads of the girls who had crawled out on the ledges to jump. The water cooled off the building and did little else.

Firemen could do little more than cool off the outside of the building. (Brown Brothers)

Battalion Chief Edward Worth, one of the first on the scene, later said that the whole situation was hopeless from the beginning. There was nothing his men could do. They had no equipment to fight such a fire. And there were no fire laws to help prevent one.

Soon after the fire had started, police units also began to arrive. The first came from the nearby Mercer Street station. One veteran of many years on the force later said that he had never seen anything like the horror that confronted him at the Asch Building.

Policemen tried to keep back the curious crowds that began to gather soon after the fire started. There was not much else the police department could do.

Ambulances came. The first was from St. Vincent's Hospital in lower New York. Doctors knelt among the fallen bodies, trying to determine if any were still alive. A number did survive the fall, only to die at the hospital. Soon a row of ambulances lined Washington Square East. One after the other, they were filled and sent off to nearby hospitals.

Word quickly spread around the city of the terrible fire that was raging in the Triangle Shirtwaist Company. People who lived in the area were brought to the scene by the screams of the girls as they jumped from windows. Those who had relatives working at the Triangle began to gather near the burning building. By 5 P.M. the police were trying to hold back a crowd of about 10,000 onlookers. By 7 P.M. the number would reach 20,000.

Within thirty minutes the fire was under control, having largely burned itself out. It was sometime after 6 P.M. when the firemen were able to enter the top three floors. They found the woodwork and window frames still smoldering. They also found the bodies of many Triangle workers. Then began the grim task of covering the victims with tarpaulins and lowering the bodies by ropes.

[38]

People waiting outside the temporary morgue to identify Triangle victims. (United Press International)

Over sixty people lay in the street. Police and firemen lined the bodies in rows and covered them with tarpaulins until the coffins arrived to take them to the morgue. A temporary morgue was set up on the pier at Twenty-sixth Street. In horrified silence, the crowd watched as body after body was taken away on horse-drawn wagons. Many followed to begin the search for missing relatives.

By early Sunday morning about forty bodies had been identified at the temporary morgue. The line of those waiting to look for friends and relatives stretched out for blocks.

Those who survived the fire suffered from burns and shock. Some of them had run out of the burning building and had not stopped until they reached their homes. Many could remember little of the horror of those few moments. For others, the horror never quite left them.

All Sunday long, crowds of New Yorkers walked slowly past the Asch Building, drawn there in silent fascination. People were still walking by on Monday. By then they had been joined by a new kind of horror. Men walked among the crowds selling jewelry and other trinkets that had supposedly been taken from the victims' bodies. It is said they did a brisk business.

After the fire was over and the building had been inspected, *The New York Times* noted that the Asch Building was in pretty good shape. The walls and floors were intact. All the floors below the eighth were relatively untouched. The building had really not suffered too badly. That, said the *Times*, was due to the fact that it was fireproof.

CHAPTER 6

Why?

Over one hundred families lost someone in the Triangle fire. In many cases, the families were newly arrived in the United States. In some cases, the girl who died had been the only one in the family who was earning any salary at all.

New York's citizens quickly began to help. Mayor William Gaynor started a money drive for the victims' families by contributing $100. The Red Cross emergency committee was ready with $5,000 by Monday morning. It provided over $100,000 altogether.

Other organizations, as well as private citizens, contributed, too. Theatrical managers gave benefit performances; the Salvation Army collected funds on the street; movie theaters donated a few days' receipts; so did the manager of a newsstand. Children sent coins; businessmen sent checks.

Most of the victims were buried during the week following the fire. It seemed for a time as though the city were filled with

Mayor William Gaynor. (United Press International)

funerals. But seven bodies were still in the morgue. They had not been, or could not be, identified.

The city announced that it would bury the unidentified bodies on April 5. Both the Women's Trade Union League and the ILGWU local union called for a memorial parade on that day.

The parade started at 1:30 P.M. in heavy rain. Over 100,000 marched in it; probably about 300,000 watched it.

[42]

The seven unidentified victims of the Triangle Shirtwaist fire were buried in a mass grave in Brooklyn. Each coffin carried a plate which read: "This casket contains a victim of the Asch Building fire. March 25, 1911."

But long before the mass funeral, the cries of protest were heard. Why had it happened? Where did the fault lie? What could be done?

Every public official, including the governor of New York, the mayor of New York City, the head of the building department, the labor commissioner, building inspectors, and others, made statements about the fire. They all agreed that it was tragic. But no one wanted any part of the blame.

Less than a month after the fire, the Triangle owners, Isaac Harris and Max Blanck, were indicted for manslaughter. They were tried for the death of just one of the victims, Margaret Schwartz, not all 146. The charge of manslaughter is used when the killing of a human being occurs without *intent* to kill, such as in an accident. It was charged that because the ninth-floor door was locked on the Washington Place side, the death of Margaret Schwartz had occurred.

In December of that year, the trial began. It lasted about three weeks. During that period, many of the surviving Triangle workers were called to testify. Testimony centered around three main points. Was the door actually locked at the time of the fire? Did the owners know that it was locked, in violation of the law, at the time? Did the victim die as a direct result of the locked door?

Justice was not served at the trial of the Triangle owners. But the outcome played an important part in the story.

Max D. Steuer, a famous New York lawyer, defended Harris and Blanck. Assistant District Attorneys Bostwick and Rubin led the prosecution. The trial was held in the old Criminal Courts Building,

[43]

Pointing to a locked door. (United Press International)

in New York, and was presided over by Justice Thomas T. C. Crain.

The state intended to prove that the Washington Place door was locked and that Margaret Schwartz's death had been a direct result of that fact. To do so, it sent to the stand witness after witness to describe what they remembered of those few horrible moments. The star witness was a young woman named Kate Alterman. She told the story of watching Margaret Schwartz trying to open the door in

[44]

question; of how the victim had screamed, "The door is locked!"; and of how she had died.

Kate Alterman's testimony was extremely damaging, and Steuer knew it. Therefore, he proceeded to discredit her, but in a quiet and gentle manner. Perhaps this was one of the greatest cross-examinations of his brilliant career.

Steuer had Kate Alterman repeat her story over and over, which she did, hardly changing a word. By the time he was through, he had left the impression that the star witness had been carefully coached by the prosecution lawyers.

When Steuer began his defense, his main objectives were to show that the door in question was always kept open and that, in any case, the Triangle owners were not aware of any violations of the law on their part.

It was obvious near the end of the trial that the prosecution witnesses had been carefully coached. It was also obvious that defense witnesses were lying. Which way would the jury go?

Judge Crain seemed to make sure of the outcome. At the trial's end, he told the jury that unless they were sure "beyond a reasonable doubt" that Harris and Blanck actually knew the door was locked at the time of the fire, the owners must go free.

And so they did. The jury took less than two hours on December 27 to find them not guilty. Harris and Blanck needed a police escort to get through the mob outside the court building.

Justice had not been served. Yet, in a curious way, the outcome of the trial assured that reforms would be made. People were outraged all over again because the Triangle owners had been permitted to go free. If they had been found guilty, the furor might have died down and the reforms might not have been so extensive.

[45]

The public had wanted something done about the Triangle tragedy. The trial made sure that something, indeed, would happen, and soon.

CHAPTER 7

The Reforms

The fire at the Triangle Shirtwaist Company changed an industry. It spurred the unions to work more responsibly for safe and sanitary conditions for garment workers. It led directly to changes in existing fire regulations and to new fire laws. In October, 1911, the Sullivan-Hoey Fire Prevention law was passed. It increased the powers of fire commissioners and organized a division of fire prevention. By 1914, three years after the Triangle fire, a commission set up to investigate factories had brought about thirty-six new labor laws in the state of New York. As a result, the state department of labor was completely changed.

But not one of these things could have happened so quickly — or perhaps so effectively — if it had not been for the public's reaction to the Triangle fire. It was people who brought about these changes. People who were horrified by the fate of 146 garment workers. People who were angry at the outcome of the trial. People who asked why. People who demanded change. People who were

Governor John A. Dix. (Brown Brothers)

determined not to let the same horror happen again. And most of all, people who did not forget.

Almost immediately after the tragedy, organizations such as the Women's Trade Union League began to demand that more be done than merely establishing the cause of the Triangle fire. Others joined in the cry for action.

So, on June 30, 1911, New York Governor John Alden Dix signed a bill to create the New York State Factory Investigating Commission. Its purpose was to look into factory conditions in the state and report on its findings by February 15, 1912. Ten thousand dollars was assigned for this purpose.

[48]

Actually, the Commission worked for two and a half years and investigated many other areas beside fire hazards. It looked into unsanitary and unsafe working conditions, labor laws concerning women and children, and others. Its lengthy report became a sort of textbook for factory reforms.

Eight men and one woman were named to the Commission. The chairman was Robert F. Wagner, Sr., then a state senator. (His son Robert years later would become mayor of New York City.) Others on the Commission included Samuel Gompers and Mary E. Dreier, president of the Women's Trade Union League.

The Factory Commission investigated over 3,500 businesses, including department stores, printing works, manufacturing shops, and canneries. In general, it found that factories were dirty and unsafe places to work. Shops were overcrowded. They were filled with cigarette smoke and combustible materials. The fire escapes were so narrow or of such poor material that they were practically useless.

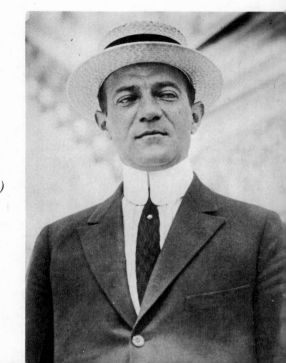

Robert F. Wagner, Sr. (Brown Brothers)

The investigators also discovered that fire claimed about one death a day in New York City.

When the Commission turned in its report, many changes were demanded in the fire and labor laws of the city and state.

Fifty percent of the fires in New York could be eliminated, said the report, if smoking laws were enforced in factories and if rubbish were carted away. (In the Triangle Company the smoking laws were largely ignored and material scraps were removed only every few months.) The report also stated flatly that the fire at the Triangle was due to a lighted cigarette thrown onto a pile of material.

Therefore, within six months, or a year in some cases, said the Commission, the New York City Fire Department should direct the placing of fireproof receptacles in all factories. All rubbish should be placed in them. *No Smoking* notices must be posted where they could be easily seen, and the rule must be enforced. All gas jets must be covered by a globe or enclosed in wire.

The New York City fire chief had made a statement that not one person would have died in the Triangle fire if the building had had a sprinkler system. Such a system consisted of a huge tank of water, usually located on the roof, with connecting pipes that ran along the ceilings. Sprinkler heads were spaced at various intervals along the pipes. As soon as the temperature reached a certain point, presumably from flames, the heads would open and the water would pour down.

The Commission said that an automatic sprinkler system had to be installed in every factory over seven stories high. It also said that every company with over twenty-five employees must hold a fire drill, supervised by the fire department, every three months.

However, the Commission would not recommend a fire alarm

[50]

The rubble that remained of the Triangle Shirtwaist Company. (United Press International)

system for employees in a factory. The members felt that a bell might panic the workers.

At the Triangle Company, the women had been crowded too closely together, the doors and windows were too narrow, and the doorways — against regulations — opened in. The Factory Commission said that there should be only fifty-five people on each floor of a nonfireproof building, and about sixty-two in a fireproof building. (This conclusion was based on a building twenty-five feet wide and eighty feet long.) Furthermore, each building with fifty people above the first floor had to post notices giving the number of people who could safely occupy each floor.

According to the new laws, windows and doors that led to fire escapes had to be at least two feet wide. They also had to be made of wired glass. And the law which called for doors to open out, said the report, must be strictly enforced.

The Factory Investigating Commission had done its work well concerning fire conditions and in other areas. It felt that all the existing laws had to be more carefully enforced. It also agreed that further investigation would show that new laws were probably needed.

The members ended their report by stating that some associations felt that as long as the Commission was investigating city conditions, it should do something about making Fifth Avenue beautiful. But this time the Commission declined. It said that it had no recommendations on cleaning up Fifth Avenue.

CHAPTER 8

Today on the Square

Many things have changed in Washington Square since 1911. It is no longer the fashionable part of the city. But it is still picturesque, with a certain special charm of its own. New York University

Washington Square today. (New York Convention and Visitors Bureau)

students sun themselves between classes; mothers push baby carriages; and old men play chess, with a crowd looking over their shoulders.

Neat-looking town houses and apartment buildings line Washington Square North and West. The buildings of New York University now occupy all of Washington Square South and East. Greene Street is still there, but the American Book Company and the Asch Building are gone. The university now takes up that entire block also.

But there is still a reminder of the Triangle fire. On the northwest corner of Greene Street and Washington Place, a bronze plaque is attached to the New York University building. It reads:

Triangle Fire

On this site, 146 workers lost their lives in the Triangle Shirtwaist Company fire on March 25, 1911. Out of their martyrdom came new concepts of social responsibility and labor legislation that have helped make American working conditions the finest in the world.

International Ladies' Garment Workers Union
March 25, 1961

A Selected Bibliography

Morris, Richard B. *Fair Trial*. New York: Harper Torchbooks, Rev. ed. 1967.

Newton, Douglas, ed. *Disaster, Disaster, Disaster*. New York: Watts, 1961.

New York State Factory Investigating Commission: *Report to the Legislature of the State of New York*. 1912.

Perlman, Selig and Taft, Philip. *History of Labor in the United States, 1896-1932*. Volume IV. New York: Macmillan, 1960.

Peterson, Florence. *American Labor Unions*. New York: Harper, 1963.

Rayback, Joseph G. *A History of American Labor*. New York: Macmillan, 1959.

Stein, Leon. *The Triangle Fire*. New York: Lippincott, 1962.

Teper, Lazare. *The Women's Garment Industry*. New York: ILGWU, 1937.

Index